Animals with Strength

Musk Oxen

by Julie Murray

Dash!
LEVELED READERS
An Imprint of Abdo Zoom • abdobooks.com

Dash!
LEVELED READERS

Level 1 – Beginning
Short and simple sentences with familiar words or patterns for children who are beginning to understand how letters and sounds go together.

Level 2 – Emerging
Longer words and sentences with more complex language patterns for readers who are practicing common words and letter sounds.

Level 3 – Transitional
More developed language and vocabulary for readers who are becoming more independent.

THIS BOOK CONTAINS RECYCLED MATERIALS

abdobooks.com

Published by Abdo Zoom, a division of ABDO, PO Box 398166, Minneapolis, Minnesota 55439. Copyright © 2023 by Abdo Consulting Group, Inc. International copyrights reserved in all countries. No part of this book may be reproduced in any form without written permission from the publisher. Dash!™ is a trademark and logo of Abdo Zoom.

Printed in the United States of America, North Mankato, Minnesota.
102022
012023

Photo Credits: Getty Images, Minden Pictures, Shutterstock
Production Contributors: Kenny Abdo, Jennie Forsberg, Grace Hansen, John Hansen
Design Contributors: Candice Keimig, Neil Klinepier

Library of Congress Control Number: 2022937233

Publisher's Cataloging in Publication Data

Names: Murray, Julie, author.
Title: Musk Oxen / by Julie Murray
Description: Minneapolis, Minnesota : Abdo Zoom, 2023 | Series: Animals with strength | Includes online resources and index.
Identifiers: ISBN 9781098280048 (lib. bdg.) | ISBN 9781098280574 (ebook) | ISBN 9781098280871 (Read-to-Me ebook)
Subjects: LCSH: Muskox--Juvenile literature. | Cattle--Juvenile literature. | Muscle strength--Juvenile literature. | Cattle--Behavior--Juvenile literature. | Zoology--Juvenile literature.
Classification: DDC 599.647--dc23

Table of Contents

Musk Oxen 4

More Facts 22

Glossary 23

Index 24

Online Resources 24

Musk Oxen

Musk oxen live where it is cold! They are found on the **Arctic tundra**.

5

Musk oxen are large animals. They can weigh up to 800 pounds (363 kg).

They stand five feet (1.5 m) tall. They can be eight feet (2.4 m) long.

Musk oxen have short legs. Their bodies are big and strong.

They have a thick skull. Their horns are curved. These are used for protection.

Males **butt** heads. The force of this is strong! It can be heard a mile (1.6 km) away.

Musk oxen have two layers of thick fur. This keeps them warm!

They have strong hooves. They use their hooves for digging. They find food in the frozen ground.

Musk oxen eat plants. In winter, they mainly eat **moss** and roots. In summer, they feed on grass and flowers.

More Facts

- Musk oxen are closely related to sheep and goats.

- They communicate through grunts, bleats, and roars.

- They are named for their strong, **musky** smell.

Glossary

Arctic tundra – a tundra biome located in the northern hemisphere near the North Pole. The Arctic is known for its cold, desert-like conditions.

butt – to hit or push with the head or horns.

moss – a small, green plant without flowers that grows in soft, thick clumps. Moss often grows in mats on rocks, trees, and wet ground.

musky – smelling of or resembling musk. Musk is a substance with a strong smell that is made by the gland of certain male deer.

Index

Arctic 4

body 11

food 18, 20

fur 17

habitat 4

hooves 18

horns 13

legs 11

males 14

size 6, 8, 11

skull 13

strength 11, 14, 18

Online Resources

To learn more about musk oxen, please visit **abdobooklinks.com** or scan this QR code. These links are routinely monitored and updated to provide the most current information available.